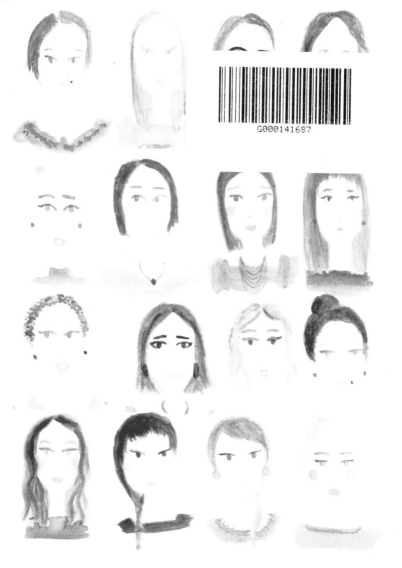

G000141687

What my girlfriends told me

FOR MUM AND DAD,
WHO TAUGHT ME I CAN BE WHATEVER
I WANT TO BE. IF I WORK HARD ENOUGH.

WHAT MY GIRLFRIENDS told ME

SONJA BAJIĆ

1 3 5 7 9 10 8 6 4 2

First published in 2018 by September Publishing

Text and illustration copyright © Sonja Bajic 2018

The right of Sonja Bajic to be identified as the author of
this work has been asserted by her in accordance with
the Copyright Designs and Patents Act 1988.

Cover and page design by Sonja Bajic and
Martin Brown

Printed in and bound by
L&C Printing Group

ISBN 978-1-910463-79-6

September Publishing
www.septemberpublishing.org

I was sitting on the Paris Métro, going home from work. My eyes were crying. I say my eyes, because actually I was perfectly OK, except my eyes – they were irritated and tears were running down my face for three or four stations. I was reading something and wiping them off. The Métro stopped at the station close to my house. I jumped out and I started walking towards the exit.

A girl tapped me on my shoulder. I looked at her. She made a heart using her hands. Confused, I pointed back at myself. *A heart for me?* She nodded and made a hand-heart sign once again. I smiled vaguely. She left. I said loudly, '*Merci*'; she waved affirmatively, without turning her head.

I walked home smiling.

It's somewhere after midnight and the night is warm – probably the first warm night of the season. I am walking slowly down the old dark street. I know the street, I feel safe, home is near. Two girls are passing by me. One is crying; her friend is hugging her and telling her soothing words. The non-crying one stops me and asks me if I have a Kleenex. I am surprised that I am being stopped – it's too late and too dark, people don't communicate often with strangers at this hour – but I am taking out my Kleenex packet with a drawing of a cartoon *Frozen* on it, I am giving it to the crying girl and I smile.

Big cities like Paris don't put you in these situations – you are usually left to laugh your own laugh or fight your own misery, but here . . . I was a witness and an accomplice to this small emotional whirlpool. Out of nowhere I became a part of their tribe, and I felt like I needed to say something – like I needed to give my fair share of soothing words to the crying girl in front of me, and not just a handkerchief. I told her that, 'Everything will be just fine *when* you clear your head up – things look much sillier now than they will look in the morning.' I also added that, 'He probably wasn't worth that MAC mascara that is running down your cheeks.' I told her what I got in similar situations from my girlfriends, my very personal tribe. I told her a simple truth, some simple well-known facts, something easily applicable to whatever situation she was fighting in the midst of the night and in drunken half-reality.

I was not sure if the girl understood me. I had decided to stick to safe ground and English for my little borrowed wisdom. She looked at me while wiping her tears, her non-crying friend looked at me and they gave me a nod and a timid smile. I said it again in French, and they nodded again. As they were walking away I heard them explaining to each other what I said, and then from the dark background of my walk home I heard one loud and one husky, '*Merci*'. I waved affirmatively.

I just knew I had to respond with something – to tell her that '*everything* will be OK'. This 'OK' can come in many shapes and forms. I am always more than happy to participate in the 'it will be OKs' of my friends and family, and I am lucky enough to have friends and family who want to participate in mine. I am also lucky enough to always be surrounded by amazing women – women who do not take no for an answer, women who fight their fights, who stay proud in front of danger, who believe in education and emancipation, women who support and who are worthy of being supported, and women who are ladies in every situation. Above all – I am lucky to be surrounded by women who know how to make simple, everyday life worth celebrating.

Words from my mother, grandmothers and aunts gave a lot of structure to the woman I've become. My first big 'no parents allowed' vacations were with four girls. An Italian lady friend of mine got me hooked on illustration – making my reality totally different today. When I moved to Paris, there was a woman who let me stay with her for free and helped me find a good place of my own. Later I met that one lady friend who would support me today in 99 per cent of things (and who often stops me being a clown); I became her wedding witness.

My support system has been built from people of all five continents, and one cat. I tried to count nationalities of my friends and family – and there are simply too many. Each of them has brought something that has made me rethink my position, made me look wider and further. I am grateful for that. My lovely Brazilian friend, Renata – an ally from the moment she lent me her hand cream in the heat of the Calabrian summer – taught me the secrets of her South American aunt. Lily, a lady from Oxford, with whom I have a glass of white wine every now and then on Saturdays, after the market, always underlines how expecting the best you deserve and fighting for that 'best' is always necessary. I was standing on the roundabout on Bastille with Annie from Minnesota one day, aching with heartache and *weltschmerz* and god knows what else . . . I have captured all her American positivity in this book as well. Some of these mind-blowing phrases I got in late-night messages from Australia, minutes after I turned down a job offer that undervalued my skills, education and personality. Many of these sentences are about new beginnings – in this or that way – and hopefully there is something that is applicable to any situation you might find yourself in.

I've been a lifetime gatherer of lovely phrases and good stories. Some of those words pulse in my head at certain instants. Some of them were always and forever with me because they came in the moment of big changes; some of these words came from the depths of my memory and from what I was taught as a child. Others I found on the margins of my past journals and notebooks – written in green, gold, neon pink, almost erased graphite, very small and very big. These words were written down over long phone conversations or in the midst of an inspiring discussion or a boring lecture. They were written often on drawing paper, but also on other people's business cards. Anything was the right canvas for the right words at the right moment; I had an urge to scribble them down and I did. While compiling this book, I went through dozens of conversations with important friends on Facebook Messenger, through Instagram conversations, old emails, text messages, Viber and Skype and WhatsApp.

Words are soothing and encouraging. Right words in the right moment can kill days of heartache. Right advice in the right moment can save you so much trouble. And the right anti-age cream recommendation can save your face so many lines. Having a support system that is there when your days are short and your nights are long is sometimes the best thing you can have. I am very grateful for these words of advice I got along the road. I am hoping those words will give you, too, a small – but often very needed – push.

In truth, there are actually a few phrases in this book I got from my male friends. It's not important which. Those men cared enough and that is why their phrases of wisdom are female enough to be here.

Recently, I went home to Serbia for some advice from my wise parents and some good food. I slept in my parents' home and had a long late-night conversation with my sister, Senka . . . the next morning, I woke up and there was a message on the mirror in the bathroom written on a Post-it note: 'Do whatever you can to make this day *better*', with 'Senka' written underneath in small letters. You'll find this advice among the pages of this tribute to the longest relationships in our lives – friendship.

JUST BECAUSE YOU DON'T LIKE THE GAME,
DOESN'T MEAN THAT GAME DOES NOT EXIST.

IN YOUR HEAD, HE'S MORE INTERESTING
tHAN IN REAL LIFE.

HOW DID YOU FEEL ON tHAt DAtE?

JUST BECAUSE YOU CAN EAT ANOTHER COOKIE,
DOESN'T MEAN YOU SHOULD EAT ANOTHER COOKIE.

EAt ANOTHER COOKiE.

IT'S PRETTY OFTEN BETTER to BE
THAN to HAVE.

ONE OF THE BEST THINGS YOU CAN LEARN
IS to KNOW WHEN YOU ARE TRYING too HARD.

MY FRIEND'S AUNT FROM BRAZIL ONCE SAID:
ALWAYS PUT SPF CREAM ON YOUR HANDS
- THAT'S THE ONLY PART OF THE BODY THAT
WILL IMMEDIATELY SHOW YOUR AGE - THERE'S
NO BOTOX FOR HANDS.

NOBODY CAN BE A JERK ALL THE TIME.

DRAMA IS USELESS. EGO IS USELESS.
DRAMA IS USELESS. EGO IS USELESS.

A REAL LADY ALWAYS CARRIES
AN UMBRELLA IN HER PURSE.

YOU NEED to PROTECT <u>YOURSELF</u> FIRST.

IT'S HARD BEING AN ADULT AND HAVING TO
BUY THINGS LIKE FURNITURE AND A CAR.
BEING ADULT SUCKS.

'INTERESTING STORY' IS NOT GOOD ENOUGH
ANYMORE. YOU WANT A GOOD STORY.

IF YOU WERE talking to ME AS YOU ARE
talking to YOURSELF — I WOULD think YOU
ARE A DRUNK, ABUSIVE PERSON, WITH NO
EMPATHY OR LOVE. PROBABLY SOME KIND OF
A DICTATOR.

WHAT'S the POINT OF that EMOTION?

HE WAS NO ONE to YOU THREE DAYS AGO.
YOU'LL SURVIVE.

PEOPLE ARE <u>LOST</u> IN THEIR OWN NARRATIVES.

SOME PEOPLE WOULD RATHER BE DEFINITELY
IN CONTROL THAN POTENTIALLY HAPPY.

THERE ARE NO BAD DATES - ONLY <u>GOOD STORIES</u>.

IF HE DOESN't RESPECT HIMSELF WHY
WOULD HE ACTUALLY RESPECT YOU?

IF YOU THINK YOU ARE _FLIRTING_,
YOU PROBABLY ARE FLIRTING.

YOU CAN'T EAT THE SAME CHEESECAKE TWICE.

It Just takes ONE.

ATTENTION IS EASY - YOU WANT <u>CONNECTION</u>.

THERE ARE 6 BILLION PEOPLE ON THIS PLANET
AND THEY ALL HATE TO BE _L_O_N_E_L_Y_ .

COCONUT OIL SAVED MY HAIR FROM EVERYTHING.

IT'S THE <u>LACK</u> OF BREEDING.

DOES HE MAKE YOU FEEL <u>GOOD</u>?

FINDING A WAY TO HANDLE A CONFLICT
IS A FORM OF FINDING <u>PEACE</u>.

FEAR IS <u>NOT</u> AN ARGUMENT.

FROM WHAt I HEARD HE tRIED to IMPRESS YOU
WITH THE FACt HE'S VACUUM CLEANING ON
SATURDAYS. KUDOS.

NOT EVERYTHING IS SUPER INTERESTING.
LIFE IS FULL OF _FILLER_ STORIES.

FUCK THE FACT THAT IF HE CALLS YOU AT 3 A.M.,
THAT'S A BOOTY CALL, BUT IF YOU CALL HIM AT
3 A.M. YOU'RE A PSYCHO AND YOU LOVE HIM.

IF HE DOESN't WANT A GIRLFRIEND, tHAt'S COOL
- tHERE ARE MANY PEOPLE WHO ACtUALLY DO.

IT'S EASY to BE SAD, It tAKES
COURAGE to BE HAPPY.

JUST PLAY It <u>COOL</u> FOR ONCE IN YOUR LIFE.

IF HE CAN'T HANDLE YOUR SHOES,
HE CAN'T HANDLE YOUR <u>PERSONALITY</u>.

IT'S A NICE DAY. MAYBE YOU SHOULDN'T RUIN IT
WITH THE DARK SIDE OF YOUR BRAIN. TURN
OFF THE THOUGHTS AND GO FOR A WALK.

SOMETIMES THINGS NEED to REACH THE POINT OF
ABSURD FOR EVERYONE TO UNDERSTAND THAT
THINGS NEED to CHANGE.

BACK IN A DAY, AN ILLITERATE MAN COULD VOTE,
BUT NOT A LITERATE WOMAN. WE ARE OBLIGED
TO EXERCISE THE RIGHT TO VOTE, IF FOR NOTHING
ELSE - THEN FOR OUR GRANDMOTHERS WHO GOT
US THAT RIGHT!

THERE ARE PEOPLE WHO DON'T WANT to BE
YOUR FRIENDS - tHEY JUSt WANt to HANG
OUt WitH YOU. YOU SHOULDN't GIVE tHEM
MORE SPACE tHAN two DRINKS . MAYBE
tHEY CAN tEACH YOU A NEW WAY to DRINK
tEQUILA . BUt tHAt'S ALL . AND tHAt'S FINE.

YOU'LL BE EQUALLY <u>HUNGOVER</u> FROM FIVE,
SO YOU MAY AS WELL HAVE THE SIXTH
<u>JÄGERBOMB</u>.

YOU THINK THAT PERSON DOESN'T LIKE YOU
-WHEN ACTUALLY IT'S YOU WHO DOESN'T
LIKE THAT PERSON.

IT'S ALL ABOUT THE TONE.

IT'S VERY DANGEROUS to BE N̲U̲M̲B̲.
IT'S VERY D̲A̲N̲G̲E̲R̲O̲U̲S̲ NOT to BE
NUMB, AS WELL.

WHO IS ASHAMED to ASK
WILL STAY HUNGRY.

SOMETIMES THINGS START SNOWBALLING - OFTEN
YOU JUST HAVE TO SHAKE HANDS WITH THE MOJO
ONCE THE MOJO FINDS YOU.

HE DEFINITELY SMILED too MUCH FOR A
NORMAL PERSON. I WAS CERTAIN HE WAS
ORGANISING ORGIES OR EATING FIRE
OR SOMETHING.

WHEN SOMEBODY GAVE UP ON YOU AND YOU
GAVE UP ON HIM OR HER - OFTEN tHE BEST
thing YOU CAN DO IS to REALLY GIVE UP.
BE CAREFUL WITH WASHING YOUR ENERGY.

THOUGHTS ARE THOUGHTS.
DEEDS ARE DEEDS.

NEVER DATE A MAN WITH <u>DIRTY</u> SHOES.

DO IT FOR THE STORY!

YOU'RE PUTTING GOALS ON SITUATIONS NO ONE
ON EARTH COULD ACHIEVE. YOU CAN'T CONTROL
THE EMOTIONS OF OTHER PEOPLE.

IT ONLY COUNTS WHAT YOU DID, HOW HARD YOU
TRIED, HOW MUCH YOU CARED AND WHO YOU
INSPIRED. THOSE ARE THE ONLY THINGS THAT
COUNT.

THAT FOURTH <u>WHISKEY</u> AND COKE LAST NIGHT WAS A MISTAKE. A BOY WHO PULLS THE <u>SWORD</u> OUT OF MY HEAD WILL BECOME A <u>KING</u>.

CURVY ONLY MEANS YOU SHOULD <u>EXERCISE</u> MORE.

THE BIG DATABASE OF GOOD DEEDS REMEMBERS
EVERYTHING. DOING NICE THINGS ALWAYS PAYS
OFF.

YOU THINK THAT YOU'RE THINKING WHAT
YOU'RE NOT THINKING. THINK <u>AGAIN</u>.

THERE IS NOTHING THAT WILL CALM YOUR
STOMACH AS WELL AS <u>MINT</u> TEA WILL.

MOST PEOPLE DON'T HAVE TASTE. THEY JUST
FOLLOW WHAT IS SUPPOSED TO BE GOOD TASTE.
IT'S THE TASTE OF THE <u>MOMENT</u>. AND IT'S
OFTEN WRONG. LIKE SHIRTS WITH HOLES
ON THE SHOULDERS OR <u>PURPLE</u> MASCARA.

WE CAN ONLY DO WHAT WE CAN.

IT'S OK TO <u>RECOGNISE</u> THAT YOUR CHOICE WAS BAD - FROM THE LIP BALM TO YOUR EX BF. THAT'S HOW YOU <u>GROW</u>.

STOP IMAGINING THAT YOU ARE BUYING A
GRAVESTONE TOGETHER. YOU'VE ONLY SEEN
HIM TWICE.

WE BUILD OUR OWN CAGES. OFTEN PEOPLE
DON'T WANT THE FREEDOM BECAUSE IT
COMES WITH COMMITMENTS.

IMAGINE A PLAY. WELL, LIFE IS MORE LIKE
AN IMPROVISED PLAY. EXCEPT THERE'S NO
WHISPERER AND NO DIRECTOR. NOBODY
TELLS YOU WHAT TO DO. AND THAT OFTEN
SUCKS.

HAVING A LONG-DISTANCE RELATIONSHIP
IS LIKE HAVING AN IMAGINARY BOYFRIEND.

I HOPE YOU WILL GEt USED to LIFE AS
It IS SUPPOSED to BE. I NEVER DID. BUt
I FOUND MY OWN BEtER WAYS.

BE CAREFUL WITH PEOPLE WHO HAVE
EVERYTHING. THEY THINK THEY CAN
HAVE YOU EASILY AS WELL.

PEOPLE DON'T WANT to CARE BECAUSE THEY
WOULD NEED to tAKE AN A<u>CtION</u>.AND PEOPLE
ARE LAZY.

I WANTED SOME THINGS THAT NEVER HAPPENED.
OR AT LEAST THAT IS WHAT I THINK I WANTED
TO HAPPEN. I DON'T REMEMBER MYSELF WORKING
ON ANY OF THAT. MAYBE I ACTUALLY DIDN'T WANT
TO DO AND BE THAT WHAT I THOUGHT I WANTED
TO DO AND BE.

MORE SELF-ACTUALISATION, MORE SELF-RESPECT
AND MORE MIND PROTECTION IS WHAT EVERYBODY
NEEDS THESE DAYS.

JUST BECAUSE SOMETHING DOESN'T FIT IN YOUR
REALITY DOESN'T MEAN IT IS NOT HAPPENING TO YOU.

I DON'T THINK THINGS 'JUST HAPPEN'. I THINK
WE CREATE CIRCUMSTANCES FOR THEM OVER
LONG PERIODS OF TIME. THEN THEY HAPPEN.

WHISKIES YOU DRINK, PROVOCATIONS YOU DON'T RESPOND TO, BANALITIES YOU STAND AGAINST, GIFTS YOU BUY, BROCCOLI YOU EAT—BE AN EXAMPLE!

ENVY CAUSES MOST OF THE EVIL IN THE WORLD.

THAT'S ONLY SOMEBODY ELSE'S OPINION.

GIVE PEOPLE CHANCES AND LET YOURSELF
BE HURT. THAT IS HOW THIS WORLD CHANGES
AND MOVES.

IT GETS _DANGEROUS_ WHEN THE ONLY THING THAT DEFINES YOUR WEEK IS THE _WEEKEND._

FINDING SOMEONE ELSE IS NOT THAT HARD.
TRYING TO FIND SOMEBODY IMPORTANT IS
ONE HELL OF A JOB.

DON't LEt THEM CHANGE YOU.

DON't BEG ANYONE to BE A PARt
OF YOUR LIFE.

THE ONLY CURE FOR THE CELLULITE IS
WATER, MASSAGE AND EXERCISE. NO
CREAM IN THE WORLD WILL HELP.

THE DYNAMICS OF BEING HUMAN ALSO
INCLUDE BEING FAT AND HAVING ACNE
AS MUCH AS THEY INCLUDE BEING GLAMOUROUS
AND EATING WHAT YOU WANT. EMBRACE ALL
ASPECTS OF THAT FRAGILITY.

FEELING UNTOUCHABLE IS FOR BEARS AND TIGERS. YOU ARE _HUMAN_. YOU SHOULD FEEL THE _EMOTION_.

YOU DON'T GET 'YOU'RE ENOUGH' FROM ANYBODY.
YOU GET IT FROM YOURSELF.

ONCE I WENT ON A DATE AND AFTER THIRTY
MINUTES AND TWO BEERS HE STARTED CRYING
AND TOLD ME HE WANTS TO LIVE IN A FAIRY-
LAND AND DATE FAIRES AND KILL DWARVES.
IT'S GOOD WHEN PEOPLE KNOW WHAT THEY WANT.
IT SAVES YOU TIME.

HOW DO YOU MISS SOMEBODY YOU DON'T EVEN KNOW? YOU MISS THE IDEA OF THAT SOMEONE.

THE BEST PARTS OF EVERYONE'S LIFE ARE THE
SPLIT SECONDS OF <u>REALNESS</u> WITH SOMEBODY.

MAGIC STARTS WHEN YOU <u>DECIDE</u> YOU ARE MAGICAL.

I KNOW THOSE THINGS WHEN I AM NOT
FEELING SAD AND LONELY.

IF THE BEST THING ABOUT YOUR <u>WORKDAY</u> IS
THE JOURNEY - MAYBE IT'S TIME TO <u>CHANGE</u>
YOUR JOB.

DON'+ LE+ +HEM MAKE YOU SMALL .

HE'S INTERESTING to YOU BECAUSE HE'S tALL.
BEING tALL IS NOt A <u>SKILLSEt</u>.

SOMETIMES THE BEST thing to DO
IS to WALK AWAY.

JUST BECAUSE YOU MISS HIM - DOESN'T MEAN
YOU SHOULD BE TOGETHER.

DON't CONFABULATE. SORRY, I SOUND LIKE WE'RE
IN 1400 ENGLAND, BUT DON't CONFABULATE.

It's NEVER too EARLY to StARt USING
HEAVY ANtI-WRINKLE CREAM.

BEING A <u>DECENT</u> HUMAN BEING IS
ACTUALLY PRETTY EASY.

HOME IS <u>WHERE</u> THE BLENDER IS.

THE ONLY THING THAT SHOULD BE FAST IS
THE INTERNET. EVERYTHING ELSE GOOD
IN LIFE CAN BE SLOW.

ONLINE DATING IS A VERY GOOD MIRROR
OF THE CONSUMERISM WE LIVE IN.
SWIPE LEFT. SWIPE RIGHT. PEOPLE ARE
NOT DETERGENTS!

THERE'S A LIGHT BLUE <u>SHIRT</u> WITH WATERMELON
RED BUTTONS. YOU <u>SEE</u> FUTURE STAIN OF WINES
ON IT. I SEE HOW WELL IT GOES WITH YOUR EYES.
YOUR MUM <u>SEES</u> HOW IT IS too THIN AND HOW
YOU'LL PROBABLY BE COLD WHEN YOU WEAR IT.
YOUR BOYFRIEND <u>THINKS</u> IT'S too TRANSPARENT.
WE ONLY SEE WHAT WE <u>EXPERIENCED</u> OR ARE
AFRAID OF.

MAYBE THIS WILL WORK!

WE ARE ALL <u>RECOVERING</u> FROM ONE too MANY COCKtAILS, tHE WRONG SHAMPOO, HEARTACHE, FEAR OF DEATH, GREASY PIZZA... WE ARE ALL IN RECOVERY.

IT'S OK NOT TO BE AROUND FOR SOMEONE
YOU ARE EVEN <u>NOT SURE</u> YOU LIKE.

YOU SHOULDN'T EXPECT GOOD THINGS BECAUSE
YOU DID _GOOD_ THINGS. YOU SHOULD DO GOOD THINGS
BECAUSE YOU'VE ALREADY GOT GOOD <u>THINGS</u>.

TRAVELLING IS A <u>SHORTCUT</u> TO EMPATHY.

I STARTED <u>SLEEPING</u> WHEN I WAS 37.

EVEN A REJECTION FROM AN <u>IDIOT</u> IS STILL
A REJECTION. YET, LET'S UNDERLINE HE'S
AN IDIOT.

I TEND NOT to JUDGE OTHER PEOPLE'S RELATIONSHIPS. IT'S HARD ENOUGH to JUDGE MY OWN.

THINGS HAPPEN WHEN YOU HAPPEN.

RICH PEOPLE OFTEN <u>FORGE†</u> WHEN
†HEY OWE YOU CASH.

IF I WAS MALE I WOULD TOTALLY HAVE
ERECTILE DYSFUNCTION.

THERE ARE PEOPLE WHO DO _IDIOTIC_ THINGS
IN ORDER TO MAINTAIN THE SELF-LIE.

IT'S ABOUT WHAT YOU <u>ALLOW</u> YOURSELF
TO HOPE FOR.

GOOD FRIENDS ARE <u>AMAZING</u> PALATE CLEANSERS.

I'M SORRY BUT I DON't UNDERSTAND MY
<u>PARSLEY</u>...It ACtS So MALE.I took PROPER
CARE OF It AND It STARTED DYING.NOW
I DON't GIVE A <u>FUCK</u> AND It'S GROWING
LIKE CRAZY,'LOOK At ME,LOOK At ME!'

EVERYBODY HAS A <u>PERSPECTIVE</u> WORTH HAVING.

JUST BECAUSE YOU'RE HAVING FUN WHEN YOU
ARE WORKING, DOESN'T MEAN THAT PEOPLE
SHOULDN'T PAY YOU WELL FOR YOUR WORK.

SOMETIMES YOU'RE ONLY FOOD FOR SOMEONE'S
EGO. RECOGNISE THE MOMENT AND MOVE ON.

I DON'T THINK YOU CAN <u>FALL IN</u> LOVE AT THE
SWINGER <u>PARTY</u>, BUT AT LEAST WE CAN GO
FOR THE FREE FOOD. GET <u>REAL</u>.

SOME PROCESSES ARE LONG AND PAINFUL. YOU
GO FOR A RUN, A MAD DOG IS BARKING AND
RUNNING AFTER YOU, SOME CREEP IS CHECKING
YOUR TERRIBLE OUTFIT, YOUR HEADPHONES
AREN'T WORKING, THE RAIN IS JUST ABOUT TO
START — BUT YOU STILL BUILD SOME MUSCLE
ON THAT RUN!

THERE'S NOTHING WRONG IN MAKING
YOURSELF LAUGH.

LIFE IS NOT A COMPETITION—IF I'M GOOD
At SOMETHING YOU CAN BE GOOD At that
AS WELL.

YOU CAN'T PARTICIPATE IN OTHER
PEOPLE'S <u>INNER</u> DIALOGUES.

BUT YOU CAN BE THERE FOR A FRIEND WHEN
THE INNER FIGHT HAPPENS TO HELP BRING
OUT THE BRIGHT SIDE.

SURE, tonight I CAN REMIND YOU NOt
to FALL IN LOVE.

THE PRESENT MOMENT IS THE ONLY CERTAIN THING.

ASIDE FROM YOUR TASTE IN MEN.
I STILL RESPECT YOU.

I AM PROUD OF YOU!

Thank you

To my editor, Hannah MacDonald, for understanding my projects and my ideas and helping me to push them to the light of the day! To all diligent fingers of September Publishing who are with me on this exciting venture. Thanks so much Charlotte! To my parents, who are the best parents one could get – thank you for all the support, encouragement, loving and pretending to understand me when not even I understood myself. To my sister, Senka, for her sobriety, strength and endless cat video support. To Bilja and Willi for believing in me. To Maisie, who is that one friend who always makes the difference – thank you 1,000 times! To Zach, who asked me what I wake up for in the morning – the best question I have ever had. To Ilma and the Balkan Food Truck Monologues series, for always reminding me where I'm from and where I'm going to. To Simon for Ubers, Japanese whisky and respect. To Bane, who is always there to make things real. To Jess and Emma, for giving me so many great ideas for the book and life. To Zorana, for appreciation and 'go girl' attitude. To Preston for brainstorming on life. To Jela, for being a partner in crime. To Eimear for 'the star' thing and endless postcards delivery. To Lucia for being always there for me. To Stephane, Anna, Antoine and the Bottleshop crew for all the Moscow Mules and Dark and Stormys. To Danka for being an archi-girlfriend. To Francesca for showing me what I can do! To my Paris: Delia and Vincent, Mathieu, Annie, Joel, Sam, Olivier, Luciola, Mariana, Steph, Alex and Lily, Miguel and Zsanett, Jasper and Mimi, Shelley, Astrid, Sara and Boki, Mel, Lisa, Anna, Costi, Julia, Bemi . . . And my Novi Sad: Laki, Duca, Simona, Sale, Ina, Boren, Marko, Borko, Ivana T., Indji, Rade; to my Bezec crew and Marina. This book would never have happened if not for all my dear, dear friends who were there for me to laugh the loudest and cry the saddest. You might find yourself among the lines of this book and I am very grateful for your presence in my life!

Sonja Bajić was born in 1985 in Yugoslavia. While never leaving her street, she changed her country four times. Sonja uses the stories she hears, writes or loves to create all kinds of drawings and illustrations. Her architectural background is often reflected in her love for maps that she also draws on a daily basis.

Today, after living in Serbia, Italy and Germany, Sonja works from Paris, France. She's been up the Eiffel Tower 694 times.

www.sonjabajic.com